LET'S PLAY
Noah's Ark

Words and pictures by Leon Baxter

A LION BOOK

God said to Noah, ''There's going to be a flood. I want you to build a big boat, called an ark.''

God told Noah to fill the ark with two of every kind of animal.

Noah and his family went into the ark. They took plenty of food.

It rained very hard and the world was flooded. But Noah and his family were safe.

The rain stopped, the flood went down and the ark landed on top of a mountain.

Noah sent out a dove to see if the water had gone down. It came back with an olive twig in its beak.

So Noah and his family and all the animals came out of the ark.

God made a rainbow as a sign that the world would never be flooded again.

Help your child get more from this book

As well as reading this book aloud, why not encourage your child to try acting out the story?

Help your child think about their "part". How might it have felt to be one of the characters? What facial expression would they have had? What body language might they use? What might they have said? Use the child's understanding of a human character as a starting point to talk about the place of God in the story.

The picture at the start of this book shows some of the basic "props" needed to act out this story. Their use can be seen in each of the changing scenes of the book. These are only suggestions. If the right materials are not available most children will be happy to improvise.

If you have some time to spare, you can easily create simple support materials that will make acting the story more fun. Why not encourage your child to help with these? (The same materials could be used for Sunday school or classroom play.) Here are some ideas:

- Collect boxes of various sizes, the largest to be the ark, the smaller ones to add to the available range of animal toys.
- Cut out two of several different animals to go into the ark box.

- Rations are important. Use biscuits or, if time permits, make some rolls and loaves of salt pastry dough, baked slowly until hard. (These are not for eating.)

- Collect empty cereal boxes, food packets and bags to load into the ark.

- As an alternative to scattering pieces of paper you can thread silver foil pieces onto woollen threads or strings, knotted at one end and suspended from a stick. Several held high and moved around will make a convincing shower of rain.

- Put some rice into empty plastic bottles and shake to make the sound of falling rain.

- Make a large, beautiful rainbow. It can be painted or made from screwed-up tissue paper stuck onto a paper arc.

The children can dance and sing to celebrate when the flood goes down. They can be told that the rainbow reminds us of God's love for his people and his promise never again to send a flood over the earth.

Story text and illustrations copyright © 1995 Leon Baxter
This edition copyright © 1995 Lion Publishing
Additional material by Christine Cousins

Published by
Lion Publishing plc
Sandy Lane West, Oxford, England
ISBN 0 7459 3191 X
Albatross Books Pty Ltd
PO Box 320, Sutherland, NSW 2232, Australia
ISBN 0 7324 1205 6

First edition 1995
10 9 8 7 6 5 4 3 2 1 0

A catalogue record for this book is available
from the British Library

Printed and bound in Singapore